parenting
The MIDDLE YEARS
made *easy*

parenting

The MIDDLE YEARS

made *easy*

A BAG OF TRICKS

APPROACH TO PARENTING

THE 6-12 YEAR OLD

ANNA COHEN

To order additional copies of this book, contact:
Xlibris Corporation
1-800-618-969
www.Xlibris.com.au
Orders@Xlibris.com.au
501030

Contents

To my daughters Abbi and Claudia

Acknowledgements

The completion of this book would not have been possible without the endless support and deep love of my family. I thank Michelle Ingram and Nerolie Muller for their gentle care, guidance and motivation to take on extra work in addition to their already overloaded and hectic schedules. Thank you as well to my dear friends, particularly Tash Rumble for her editorial input and Kelly Holcroft for her artistic prowess and endless willingness to 'workshop' this project. Your patience and generosity is greatly appreciated. Lastly I would like to thank all the children and families who I have been privileged to work with over the years. You have been my inspiration.

> We want more for our children than healthy bodies. We want for our children to have lives filled with friendship and love and high deeds . . . We want them to be eager to learn to be willing to confront challenges . . . We want them to grow up with confidence in the future, a love of adventure, a sense of justice. We want them to be resilient in the face of the setbacks and failures that growing up always brings.
>
> Seligman (1995: 6) The Optimistic Child.

Introduction

The information contained in these pages is designed to be a 'bag of tricks' for you to use with kindness in your parenting. These strategies are not intended to be the magic solution to all your difficulties and may need to be changed slightly to suit your family or your own way of speaking. The ideas in this book have worked for thousands of families, but they are examples and suggestions only. Remember, you're the one who knows your family inside out and that by being clear in your expectations, you can make your parenting role easier.

Most of us have trained for our chosen career, but we assume that the job of a parent requires no schooling. At times, we blindly navigate this process in an unplanned and reactive way, often making up our rules or better still our expectations and strategies as we go along. Our job as a parent is hard work. It challenges our competence, our energy, and our emotions. Parenting questions our ability to establish firm, consistent, clear, predictable, and yet loving boundaries. Children will always test out how elastic these boundaries are and how far they can be stretched. This is a normal part of growing up and is how a child gets ready to be in charge of their life as an adult. All children will be 'hard work', 'difficult', or 'challenging' at times. This book is intended to give you a 'bag of tricks' to use with your child to help you navigate this challenging territory with assertiveness, decisiveness, confidence, empathy and compassion.

The strategies advocated are designed to direct as opposed to control children and stem from the acknowledgement that children, by virtue of being children, will make behavioural errors. Remember, children are not mini adults. They are egocentric, and their behaviour is at times thoughtless and impulsive. It is a myth to think that they should be well behaved and always do as they are told. As Louise Porter (2001) reminds us, if we punish children for acting thoughtlessly, impulsively, or carelessly, then we would be punishing them for being children.

This book contains ideas that are powerful and appeal to children's pride, reason, logic, and concern for others whilst teaching the expression of negative emotions in appropriate ways. When all the strategies in this book come together—describing and validating feelings, acknowledgement, effective instruction delivery, consequences, planned ignoring and noticing the positives—children will notice several big changes.

Firstly, their home life will be more peaceful and less conflictual. There will be less shouting, fewer threats, fewer unanswerable questions, and less guilt placed on them. This means they will not feel bombarded or like they are hurting anyone by their actions. They will be less anxious because they will not worry about their relationship with their parents and about being a 'bad' or 'naughty' person.

Secondly, they will feel more secure and unconditionally loved and accepted. Children may squirm and dismiss the positive things that you say, but that doesn't stop the positive impact on their sense of self. They will feel like you believe in them and that the little things that they do get noticed. This will help them to believe in themselves and as such they will want to do them more often.

Thirdly, children will still make mistakes, but you will not see that they have to be rescued from their mistakes. Children will notice the adults in their lives doing exactly what they said they would and neither getting wound up nor giving in when they meet resistance. They will see their parents setting clear limits while listening receptively to their requests and questions.

It is normal that children will not initially like new structures. They will test the rules, beg, get angry, blame, play on your emotions, and any other number of creative techniques. Ultimately, they will recognise that old patterns of behaviour are no longer effective, and will be drawn to take on their new responsibilities with grace and cooperation. In doing so, children will feel more competent and worthwhile. They will notice changes in the way their family spends time together—chatting, laughing, and enjoying interacting on occasions that used to be the most stressful and conflictual. This picture may sound unrealistic, but it is absolutely achievable. Many parents and carers have developed their bag of tricks and found that these methods significantly improve their family's daily life.

Finally, the strategies in this book all take time and hard work. But it is worth it. Parents notice big changes at home after only a few weeks. They report feeling confident and equipped, with their children being more in control of their feelings and more inclined to do the right thing.

Chapter 1

Principles of parent management

All children need to feel a sense of dignity and competency. Our job as parents and responsible caregivers is to encourage the greatness of our children. We do this by acknowledging their intelligence and initiative, enhancing a sense of fun and play, and giving them the skills to be able to show empathy and care for others. Through the mastery of these skills children are able to develop their own knowledge of right and wrong, an inner conviction of wanting to do the right thing, and the confidence to act on this knowledge. Through compassionate and assertive parenting we facilitate the successful development of a child's window of tolerance for learning and for managing the ups and downs of life. This window is a child's ability to react and not overreact to daily events and is ultimately the ability to think and feel at the same time.

In order for children to develop considerate behaviour, they need to have a large window of tolerance. To develop this, children need to learn to:

- cooperate with others
- have a strong sense of self-efficacy, that is, a belief that they have the skills and ability to succeed in certain situations

- have good self-discipline and an inner sense of knowing right from wrong
- have autonomous ethics, that is, for children to have developed a system of beliefs that help them think about their own behaviour and its effect on others and so they make good, pro-social choices even when a situation is new to them and no-one has told them what to do.

As parents, it is our job to cultivate confidence, perseverance, resilience, accountability, social adaptability, and a spacious and flexible window of tolerance in our children. We need to demonstrate and model communication that is respectful so that the children in our charge can learn to behave considerately with their peers now and during their development into their adult selves. Considerate behaviour is not about children just doing as they are told. It requires that children learn to think about the effects of their behaviour on themselves and others rather than the chance of being caught or the likely punishment to themselves.

Developmental needs

By understanding how children develop, we can establish fair and reasonable expectations for them while finding effective strategies and tools to teach and nurture successfully. The development of a child's self-esteem is reliant on multiple factors. These factors include their sense of belonging in their environment, their feelings of personal safety and how they experience self-efficacy. Self-efficacy is their experience of personal competence and mastery. All of these help create a child's sense of identity. Children with strong self-esteem and sense of self-efficacy not only know right from wrong but also believe that they are capable of successfully acting on that knowledge.

Satisfaction with who we are and how we are loved is an essential part of a happy and fulfilling family life and the foundation from which optimal child development flows. Children and young people need to feel safe, secure, loved, and know that their parents and caring adults will have clear expectations, make fair requests and set appropriate limits on their behaviour.

It is a normal part of life for us all, both children and adults, to feel resentful, jealous, inadequate, abandoned, let down, and left out at times. When we experience these strong feelings of hurt and disappointment, we can be tempted to react critically. However, shaming and blaming actually leads to more upset. When we share our feelings and feel understood and listened to, our relationships become stronger, and we feel loved, empowered and valued.

Children between the ages of six and twelve master a range of competencies, including developing through mistakes they make, learning to accept and respect family expectations, and understanding concepts of cause and effect through considerate behaviour (how behaviour effects others). They also learn about cooperating and being able to accept that even the people we love the most may not always agree with us (or with each other). Throughout this developmental stage children often act in ways that are more challenging to parents. For example they may increasingly show their resentment of parental requests and become more testing of family limits and expectations. All of this can be expected to result in increased arguing with parents.

As parents, there are many things that we can do to assist our children as they develop in this period of their life. We need to allow them to develop and understand responsibility. This can be through assigning small jobs or chores around the house, making them aware of expectations and the routine for both themselves and the family, as well as allowing them to experience consequences. Allowing consequences to occur helps children to learn to be accountable for their actions. While responsibility is important, it is crucial that expectations are a good match for your children's age and capability so that we are not expecting too much from them. Children also need us to nurture their minds and their souls through providing honest answers to the questions that they ask and always ensuring that they feel safe.

Characteristics of the child during the middle years

Job of the six to twelve-year-old child

—Learn new skills and learn from their mistakes
—Practice thinking and doing
—Know family expectations and why they are important
—Experience fair and logical consequences of inconsiderate behaviour
—Disagree with others and have their own opinions (and still be loved)
—Test ideas and values
—Develop self-control
—Learn about responsibility
—Develop the capacity to cooperate with others
—Develop a spacious window of tolerance, that is, the ability to think and feel at the same time

---

Typical behaviours of the six to twelve-year-old child

—Ask questions and gather information
—Practice and learn skills
—Compare, test and experience consequences
—Challenge the values of their parents

Helpful parent behaviour

—Encourage children to engage in and master their developmental tasks
—Offer love, safety, protection, and support
—Support a child's efforts to try to learn to do things their own way
—Be a source of inspiration
—Be clear about children's responsibilities
—Set fair and clear boundaries, routines and expectations
—Allow children to experience consequences and how to repair/ restore relationships
—Respond positively to children's curiosities
—Listen to the messages behind children's words
—Be respectful
—Focus on teaching
—Model manners and empathy for others
—Lead their family through guidance
—Adapt expectations to their child's capabilities

Building your bag of tricks

This bag of tricks approach is aimed at reducing opportunities for damaging expressions of parent-child conflict and encouraging cooperative relationships within your family. The bigger your bag, the more likely you are to see the behaviours that you want to see and less of those that are unproductive. This approach will not only let your child know that you see when they are frustrated or angry but also show them effective ways to deal with these often intense feelings. Ultimately these strategies will assist you in setting reasonable limits and expectations and give you the skills that you need to respond quickly when limits are exceeded.

The key to building your bag of tricks is to:

1. Choose an achievable goal

Pick your most frustrating behavioural problem to concentrate on first. Don't try to change everything at once. Solve one issue before moving on to your next target behaviour.

2. Be consistent

As much as possible, all the adults, who care for the children at home, need to agree to use the same strategies in the same way and back each other up. This is crucial as mixed-up parenting encourages children to behave inconsiderately.

3. Persist

Select a few strategies from this book that you think would work for the target behaviour that you have chosen. Concentrate on putting your new ideas in place for *at least one to two weeks* before you move the goal posts or add different goals.

4. Be kind to yourself

For most parents, new strategies are hard work at first, but after a few weeks, they become habit; you won't really have to think about them too much, and you will be ready to add more tricks to your bag.

5. Stay positive

Change can take time, and with learning anything new, it can take two to four weeks for you to become comfortable with and consistently use these strategies.

6. Believe in your child

Children can take two to six weeks to really learn their new way of functioning and for old habits to be replaced by more constructive and appropriate strategies for getting their needs met.

7. Believe that change is possible

Remember that although this book has lots of techniques, you know your child best, and you may have some other good ideas of your own; only change what is not working!

8. Take good care of yourself

It is difficult for you to consistently meet your child's needs if you are neglecting your own. Try to create time to relax and do an activity that you really enjoy.

Chapter 2

Building positive relations:
the scaffolding for considerate behaviour

A strong attachment relationship between children and their parents will support the development of a spacious window of tolerance and form the scaffolding on which parent management techniques can be built. Without this we will not be effective in our management efforts. Active listening, the use of 'I' statements and the establishment of clear expectations all provide the basis to successful and assertive parenting. In fact these strategies are the most powerful of all the tricks in our bag and for many parents are the most utilised of all their tools.

Building positive relationships

The message we have traditionally given children is to do as they are told because compliance will be rewarded and bad behaviour punished. This can be defined as externally controlled. Under such control children do not develop their own sense of ethical action. It promotes not only the tendency to always need someone there to regulate behaviour, but also to continue to choose actions based on the expectation that someone else will reward or punish them later when their behaviour is known. What we are striving for is autonomous ethics or what can be termed considerate behaviour. Considerate behaviour is when a child does something because it is the right thing to do and they do not need someone there to regulate their behaviour. We want children to be considerate, not because they are afraid they might be punished or simply comply because they will get a reward, but because they know it is the right way to behave and they gain satisfaction from doing the right thing. Children who have developed autonomous ethics experience emotions such as joy and happiness when they are considerate to others and shame and regret when they are inconsiderate, regardless of feedback or direction from adults or others around them.

As adults we have a responsibility to create an emotional climate that encourages children to cooperate because they care about themselves and others. We need to demonstrate and model communication that is respectful so that they learn how to interact appropriately with their peers now and during their development into their adult selves.

Confidence

Children and young people need encouragement when they do things as well as acknowledgement to take some risks, such as joining a new dance class or sporting group. Such small experiments lead to self-confidence and pride. Alternatively, they lose confidence in their convictions and ability to run their own lives when discouraged, put-down or criticised.

Positive relationships are achievable when children feel confident and have good self-esteem. Self-esteem is protected and positive relationships are further achieved through providing constructive feedback to children. Constructive feedback is a way of describing the problem or what you see in a way that separates the behaviour from the individual ('it is not you that I do not like, it is your behaviour that is not okay') making it easier for children to hear what the problem is and deal with it. For example, saying 'dirty clothes belong in the dirty clothes basket' both describes what you see and gives children relevant information. When they act on this information they experience a sense of confidence in themselves, they come to understand that they are being trusted to make good choices. This approach gives children information to encourage their problem-solving but still protects their confidence and self-esteem.

Self-esteem

Children's self-esteem is affected by the messages they receive from their parents and caregivers. The attitude behind your words is as important as the words themselves. Children and young people thrive when the attitude around them communicates that they are trusted, and that they have the ability to make good choices. A message that conveys 'you are capable and loved' is crucial in helping children feel valued. In giving this message we let them know that we believe in them and their abilities, and at times of conflict, we trust that they will make sensible choices.

Constructive feedback

Constructive feedback is a communication approach which helps children to be clear and positive. Support children to be direct about what they want so that you can help. For example, saying to an upset child, 'Tell me what you want', 'what are you trying to tell me?' or 'tell me more quietly so I can understand what you are saying' enables open lines of communication. However, it is crucial that we do this when a child is still in their window of tolerance as communication with a totally enraged child will not be successful.

Give children in your care the chance to express their feelings, needs, thoughts and ideas in a helpful way. Try to be constructive and responsive to what they say. Remain clear about what you will do and the reasons why. When issues are non-negotiable, take time out to calm down and talk again when the atmosphere has cleared.

None of us respond well to criticism or being blamed. When this is the communication style that a child is familiar with, they are more likely to be sensitive to it. Conversations that start with 'should', 'never', and 'always' lead to defensiveness. At times of frustration and stress, it is natural for adults to want to describe a child's behaviour in absolutes such as: 'you always . . .', 'you never . . .', 'you are . . .', 'why can't you ever?' . . . Nobody responds well to 'yes but' or to qualified praise such as 'that was great, why can't you always do that.' When put-downs and acknowledgement are combined in the same breath, all your child tends to hear is the negative.

Always use constructive comments such as:

> 'What can we do to solve this problem?'
> 'I can see/hear that you are feeling angry, tell me again using your inside voice'
> 'I trust that you two can work this problem out.'
> 'Sit here and talk about it. I know that you are both capable of sorting this problem out without me.'
> 'I trust that you two can get along much better than you are right now. What can we do to make this day more fun for all of us?'

Scaffolding children's problem solving through constructive feedback teaches them that they can communicate effectively with us and be heard. It gives them the tools that will enable them to be active participants in solving the problems that confront them—now, before they develop into their adult selves and move into the complicated adult world.

For example, if children are arguing over the remote control and which television program to watch, this is a perfect time to get involved and model effective communication.

- *Quietly and with emotions in check*, walk into the room.
- *Calmly turn off the television.* Take the remote control and place it on the table.

- *Instruct the children to sit* on the couch and tell them that they may turn on the television once they 'have a plan'.
- *Explain* that they must discuss the issue and come to a mutually acceptable solution.
- *Make a few suggestions:* 'You could look through the television guide and each agree on a specific show for today or you may decide to split up and have one person watch the television in the other room. Perhaps you will decide to keep the television off and find something else to do right now.'
- *Follow this up with a supportive statement:* 'I know you both can sort this out and come up with a good solution.' If the children seem at a loss as to how to begin, you may want to stay and help guide their conversation. If at any time one of them begins to talk to you, make certain that you interrupt and say, this is between you and your brother/sister. I'd like you to talk to him/her.'
- *Stay with them until they get the hang of it* and actually begin to negotiate and discuss possible solutions and to arrive at one they both agree will work, or at least one they are prepared to try.
- *Acknowledge* all positive behaviour and attempts at conflict resolution.

Follow this same procedure with each occasion of conflict that occurs between the children. With time and practice you will begin to hear and see them using this approach without your continued input.

Teaching children to be considerate

The key aims in guiding children's development of considerate behaviour are:

1. Self-discipline

Allowing our children to become self-disciplined through teaching them right from wrong so that they can assess how their behaviour fits into these categories both before and after they have acted.

2. Healthy emotional development

Ensuring our children develop well emotionally, and are therefore able to express how they feel without upsetting others or causing them unnecessary stress.

3. Cooperation

Giving our children the skills to be able to work with others cooperatively.

4. Self-worth

Fostering a feeling of self-worth and creating positive self-esteem. If a child has a strong sense of self-efficacy, they are more likely to act upon their knowledge of right and wrong and develop autonomous ethics.

The four areas discussed above are essential ingredients in the development of considerate behaviour. These go beyond simply following the rules because they ensure that a child understands the consequence of their actions (whatever form that may come in). This goes beyond the consequence of punishment and examines their effect on other people or aspects of life.

Effective communication as a tool for teaching considerate behaviour

When managing our children's inconsiderate and problem behaviour, we must remember that they need to be taught, not controlled, in order to develop self-regulation. We need to guide children's behaviour towards being more considerate. It is natural for them to begin by acting in inconsiderate ways until their experience expands and they have been helped to think about their actions. If we began to focus on punishing them when they first act inconsiderately, we would be punishing them for something they aren't necessarily aware is wrong.

Active listening

Good communication is about more than just what you say; it also involves actively listening to what is being said to you. Children want their parents to listen. As parents, we often talk too much, albeit with good intent. We want to reassure, to give advice and to ask questions of our children. However, this can mean that our children do not turn to us when they have something important to say.

Active listening means totally focusing on what your child is saying. This includes making eye contact, nodding your head, smiling, and using feedback such as 'uh ha . . . mmmmm?' or 'I understand'. Active listening goes beyond just engaging with what the child is saying. It involves both reading a child's body language and tone of voice.

It is important that when a child is upset, we take on this listening role and let our talking take a back seat. This means fighting the urge to ask questions or make comments. In situations where a resolution or solution is hard to reach, a child needs an understanding response. This does not have to be long; a simple response of 'I understand' can be all it takes.

Active listening is about using empathy in order to understand another person's point of view. Gaining knowledge about what is normal for your child and what matters to them as they develop is important. What they find relevant will change as they grow up and thus your responses will evolve.

'I' statements

The use of 'I' statements shows children that you have feelings too. It helps parents and caregivers to remain respectful and at the same time allows them to not accept intolerable behaviour (for example, saying to an angry ten-year-old, 'I feel upset when you yell at me. I need you to talk to me calmly'). Children whose feelings are respected are likely to model the same behaviour and be more willing and able to apologise.

The attitude that overwhelms and crushes children is one that communicates, 'you're useless and always wrong, you can't do anything right. You always make poor choices, and this latest stuff up just confirms that you never do the right thing.' Words can have a damaging effect of staying with young people for a long time and become their internal self-talk (Pantley, 2000) and their default position when under stress. Everything we say can become part of our children's inner voice, whether it is positive or negative.

'I' statements are a way to talk about difficult feelings, by saying how the problem is affecting you. 'I' statements are effective due to their ability to express your feelings without putting your child down or making them feel the need to get defensive. They also avoid a more traditional blaming approach to challenging behaviour. This allows the child to change their behaviour without the feeling of resentment towards the parent. This sort of open and positive communication allows for good feelings to remain between the parent and the child.

The regular use of 'I' statements may take some time to master, especially if you use 'you' statements on most occasions. It is important that you continue to try and use 'I' statements, even if it does feel forced. In doing this, you will enable your child to understand how you are feeling as well as recognising their point of view. If your child knows how you feel, they will be better able to understand why you are acting the way you are. The 'I' statement should also decrease the likeliness of a hostile response from your child to what you are saying.

The 'I' statement formula

When describing problem behaviour, it is important to be clear and brief. By addressing one issue at a time your child knows exactly what you are concerned about.

I feel _____ (state how you feel),
'When you _____ (describe the behaviour in a factual way without judgment),
and what I'd like is_____

This formula can be reshaped depending on what works for you. In some cases, parents prefer to state how they are feeling and then go into detail about the behaviour and the effect of this. Either of these formulas will promote open communication and a better chance of resolving the problem and changing the challenging or inconsiderate behaviour; for example, 'I feel upset when you yell at me. What I need is for you to speak to me in a calm voice.'

Establishing expectations (considerate behaviour agreements) and making them work

All children need limits to know what is expected of them. Expectations are most effective when there is a small number to remember (no more than five), they are easy to follow, and they state what we want rather than what we don't want. Involving children in creating expectations also helps to ensure that they are followed. Expectations should always be stated in the positive manner (that is, describe what you *can* do, rather than what should not happen). Consequences can be applied when expectations are not adhered to, however, it is essential that these are logical, appropriate and stated positively. For example, 'you need to finish your homework before you can watch television'.

There are four key elements to consider when it comes to making expectations work. Firstly, remain consistent, as this will assist your child in knowing what to expect and creates a feeling of security. Secondly, ensure that the expectations apply to the whole house, this minimises confusion and limits the use of the excuse 'but I didn't know' or 'it's not fair I have to do this and no-one else does'. Thirdly, parents or caregiving adults must work as a team. Lastly, be clear on your expectations, so that boundaries are not elastic and unclear.

As parents we need to listen to children before applying a consequence. A straight forward and effective approach, is to simply ask, 'what happened?' As we are teaching considerate behaviour, this offers children the opportunity to make things right. For example, 'Kate you're not doing your homework, I'm disappointed because one of our agreements was that you would do your homework as soon as you get home. What happened? What are we going to do?'

Build your bag of tricks

The key principals to introducing expectations are:

- set the scene (e.g., call a family meeting, no television!)
- be clear about why you have called everyone together
- state each expectation clearly, one at a time
- seek input from your child/ren as each expectation is explained (What is their opinion?)
- once each expectation has been decided, ask your child/ren to repeat or demonstrate it
- consider writing the expectations down
- decide on the consequences for not adhering to the expectations

The key principals to teaching considerate behaviour are:

1. Awareness
Be aware of the needs of your child and respond to them when you can.

2. Guidance
Your role is to lead the family through guidance. This involves having clear expectations, routines and boundaries.

3. Acknowledgement
Acknowledge all considerate behaviour.

4. Consequences
Allow natural consequences to be used when a child acts considerately. For example, if your child says 'thank you', you may respond with 'it's my pleasure' or 'that's okay' or a sign of affection such as a smile or a hug rather than 'good girl/boy' statement.

5. Guidelines
Guidelines that categorise considerate behaviour can assist in your ability to respond and your child's understanding of why you are responding in that way. Examples of this sort of guideline could be that we tidy up after ourselves, take our plate to the kitchen or speak calmly when feeling frustrated.

6. Skill development
Remember that behavioural errors are normal. Children do not have a deep understanding of what it means to be considerate and it is our role as adults who care for children to teach this complex skill.

7. Expectations

Adapt your expectations to your child's capabilities. It is okay to move the goal posts. If you have expectations or demands that your child is not capable of achieving, it is reasonable to alter them.

8. Assertiveness

While it is natural for our children to be inconsiderate, we do not have to tolerate intolerable behaviour. If we continuously put off being assertive as we try to stay patient, we are not teaching children that what they are doing is inconsiderate, and we may end up responding in an out-of-control manner as the situation escalates.

9. 'I' statements

Explain the impact of a child's behaviour in an assertive way, using 'I' statements. This does not include the elements of blame and criticism that can come across when using 'you' statements. 'I' statements simply convey your needs and how you are feeling about your child's behaviour. An example of an 'I' statement might be, 'I feel upset when you yell at me. I need you to speak in a calm voice.'

10. Collaboration

It is important that your child learns how to work collaboratively, especially when addressing challenges; this is something you should guide your child in developing.

11. Choices

Offering your children choices is important. This can be in the choice of activity where possible, but can also be in *how* they could do a task or *when* they would like to do it, if the task inevitably must be undertaken. Limiting choice to just two options is often helpful for children to feel empowered but not burdened by responsibility.

12. Flexibility

Make sure you think through your decisions. Flexibility and changes to your choices are fine as long as your needs are still being met.

13. Assistance

As a parent, you need to assist your children in being able to control their own behaviour and self-regulate which is the foundation for a large window of tolerance. Children who tantrum are not often doing so because they don't know how to behave. The tantrum is more an expression of having a narrow window of tolerance and of them feeling overcome by emotions so that they are unable to think clearly.

When dealing with inconsiderate behaviour, the bag of tricks approach may assist you. It begins with a management-decision chart, which is your own set of guidelines or expectations in regard to considerate behaviour. Your management-decision chart can then be acted upon when your child exhibits inconsiderate or challenging behaviour. With a bag of tricks approach you are more able to determine why problem behaviour is happening. You will have the tricks to consciously decide to either act or let the behaviour go. With your bag of tricks you will be able to be clear on why you choose to let behaviour go, such as the awareness that the problem will solve itself, your inability to feel as though you can deal with it effectively at the time, or the fact that while the behaviour isn't good, it is not going to be targeted this week. If you choose to act, you will be equipped with a solid bag of tricks such as: active listening, planned ignoring, choice statements, logical consequences, cool down or the calming strategy.

Chapter 3

Acknowledging desirable behaviour

Children's dependency on affection and approval often translates into an immense need for attention from their parents and significant others. Children strive for attention whether it is positive or negative; when attention is rare, they may see any attention as better than none at all. The attention-gaining techniques we see children display are subconscious, outside their awareness, and can become a habit very quickly.

Parents also have behaviour that they are unaware of. As parents our response to children's behaviour trains them to respond to situations in different ways. For example, if a child usually shares with their sibling and you fail to acknowledge this and only respond negatively when they don't share, then you are unintentionally training your child that it is negative behaviour that will gain your attention. Forgetting to notice the positives and focusing heavily on the negatives is easy to do and leads to conflict in the parent-child relationship. Breaking this negative cycle by acknowledging desirable behaviour is the job of parents when utilising this bag of tricks approach.

Through the acknowledgement of considerate behaviour children learn what is expected and they internalise the right way to behave. In the previous example, by recognising the child's sharing with a simple thank you and then asking them how they felt and how they think their sibling felt, the child is helped to gain an internal understanding of their considerate behaviour. Having a growing sense that sharing is the 'right thing to do' and an awareness that it 'makes them (and others) feel good' over time lessens the need for acknowledgement from others. This acknowledgment also allows the child to see that their considerate behaviours are seen and appreciated by their parents.

Effective acknowledgement

Paying attention to behaviours increases the likelihood that you will see them more often. As such, acknowledgement is one of the most powerful ways to influence your child's behaviour. It is also an important way to help a child grow in confidence and self-esteem.

Children need frequent acknowledgement so that they learn what considerate behaviour is. Acknowledgement can be either general or descriptive. General acknowledgement is vague (e.g., 'that's great', 'good boy', 'well done') and doesn't convey to the child what they have done or how it has impacted upon anyone else. Descriptive or labeled acknowledgement is clear and specific. It tells your child exactly what it is that they have done (e.g., 'thank you for coming to the table when you were asked', 'well done for keeping your hands and feet to yourself', 'thank you for calming down and using your words'). These statements help children to change their behaviour because they indicate exactly which behaviours are appropriate.

To effectively acknowledge your child, you need to catch them behaving considerately—even if it is only for a small moment in a long period of undesirable behaviour.

Ways to acknowledge

Acknowledge your child for doing something positive with simple words and your body language; a smile or saying, 'that was a really nice thing you just did sharing with your sister.' Be wary of the temptation to reward your child for considerate behaviour with material things. By simply acknowledging their behaviour, you are making them feel noticed and validated. Children are quick to notice acknowledgement that is insincere or over the top and it can at times have an unintentional negative effect.

The application of acknowledgement allows children to know what the positive behaviour was, and the attention from doing it will make them want to repeat it. Sometimes acknowledgement can feel clichéd or unnatural. Finding your own phrases or terms that you feel comfortable with will ensure that your acknowledgement remains sincere. The following ideas may help you to create your own statements to use with your child/ren.

Labelled acknowledgement ideas

The more often you acknowledge the positive actions of your child, the more likely they are to understand what it is you expect of them. As a result, you are more likely to see more considerate behaviour and less behavioural errors. As parents, we need to understand that everything we say can be internalised by our children. This is especially important when we use labels to convey expectations. If we label our child as naughty enough times, they will begin to believe it and will act accordingly. Labeling behaviour can also be a positive tool. If we consistently tell our child that they are caring or helpful, they will continue to practice traits identified with this.

It is important that we steer away from statements such as 'they should be doing it anyway, so therefore I don't need to acknowledge it'. This

omething we would not appreciate ourselves and
ke with our children who are still learning and
this positive teaching is not simply about confirming
aviour, but rather encouraging them to continue to behave
erately and develop strong self-esteem and autonomous ethics.

'I was so proud at the way you cared for your little brother today.'

'Thank you for packing away your toys without me reminding you.'

'Thank you for coming to the table straight away.'

'It's a pleasure to chat with you when you use your gentle voice.'

'You did a great job of remembering to brush your teeth before hopping into bed.'

'Thank you for sitting at the table.'

'You're doing a great job of paying attention.'

'Thank you for sharing.'

'You're being kind sisters.'

'Thank you for taking turns.'

'You're doing a great job of speaking with an inside voice.'

'Thank you for staying quiet and listening.'

'You are drawing very carefully.'

'Thank you for waiting for your turn.'

'I am really impressed with how well you are doing at . . .'

'You are really following the instructions there with your craft; that's hard to do.'

'It's a pleasure to walk into this lovely, neat room.'

'I am very moved by your poem.'

'Thank you for staying calm, using your quiet voice and keeping your hands to yourself.'

'Thanks for clearing the table.'

'You got dressed without me having to ask you, thanks.'

'Thanks for letting your sister have the last . . .'

'You did a great job helping me to . . .'

'Thank you for walking in the shop.'

'Great job of making your bed by yourself.'

Children, especially those with low self-esteem, may not always find it easy to internalise our acknowledgements. As such it can be powerfully reinforcing for them to overhear you telling another person about their behaviour ('I was so proud watching Kate being such a kind sister today'), or for another person to comment to them at a later time about what they have heard said about their considerate behaviour ('your mum told me that you did great in the school concert today, I'm so proud of you'). You can use family members such as partners, grandparents or other adult friends to practice this method of acknowledging considerate behaviour.

Be consistent

Remember behaviours that receive attention increase. Pick three or four target behaviours and get ready to 'catch' your child doing them:

Commonly desired behaviours may include:

—Helping others
—Doing good listening
—Using a pleasant voice
—Taking care of personal belongings
—Being friendly, cheerful and interested in others
—Following instructions
—Keeping hands and feet to yourself
—Playing nicely or sharing
—Getting on with others
—Telling the truth
—Taking 'no' for an answer
—Playing independently

Building your bag of tricks

How acknowledgement can be made effective

1. Awareness

When we think about acknowledgement and its effectiveness, it is important to understand two key elements. The first part is when a parent expresses how they feel about something that their child did; for example, 'I felt so proud seeing you share with your sister like that'. The second is when children can then internalise this acknowledgement and begin to praise themselves; for example, 'I'm really good at sharing, especially with my sister'.

2. More positive attention, less negative attention

Think about the behaviour(s) you want to see more of from your child and catch them doing them. If your child does not usually comply with your instructions straight away, praise them any time you notice them moving towards this behaviour or pausing to 'draw breath' in their undesirable behaviour; for example, 'Great job, you started to pack away your toys' and 'thank you for using a calm voice'.

3. Make a list

Write down some labelled acknowledgement statements that you could use to target the behaviours that you would like to see more of from your child.

Chapter 4

Encouraging desirable behaviour

Children need one-on-one time with their parents. Child-centered time does not have to be for long periods, but it must be spent between just you and your child doing something they enjoy. Interruptions should be avoided, as the aim of this process is for your child to have your complete and undivided attention. Having this one-on-one time regularly will limit your child's need to gain attention by engaging in negative and inconsiderate behaviour.

Child-centred time

Child-centred time can be both structured and unstructured. Parents can spend a lot of time and effort thinking of special activities or events they can do with their child, when often the simple things can be most effective. Special time can be to just sit with your child and listen to them read, play a board game or draw pictures. Remember it's the time spent together that is the focus, not the activity.

Structured child-centred time involves setting aside five to ten minutes of intensive time or play with your child, where they lead the activity by choosing *what* they would like to play with or do and *how* they'd like to play it. Your role is to join in, encourage and acknowledge appropriate and considerate behaviour. It is important to avoid giving instructions ('It's best if you do it like this'), asking questions ('Why have you done this, what are you doing, are you having fun') or criticising ('I can't believe you like to watch that').

There are many benefits of giving a child attention when you are able. Often it means they will be less likely to demand attention when you are not able to give it. Child-centred time strengthens the relationship between a child and parent, making them feel secure and creating the foundation for dealing with conflict and inconsiderate behaviour. The one-on-one attention also tends to improve children's language development, play skills and concentration span. Many parents find that through child-centred time their children gain more ideas about how to play and are able to spend more time entertaining themselves. Ultimately this time improves children's self-esteem and self-worth.

Child-centred time takes practice. Most parents find these bag-of-tricks strategies difficult to apply at first—engaging in child-centred playtime is not easy. As adults, it is hard not to ask questions and easy to miss opportunities to acknowledge and encourage. Don't be discouraged. As with any new skill, it takes time and practice.

Building your bag of tricks

How to make structured child-centred time effective

Step one
Decide on a time each day that will be your 'special' time with your child. Aim to set aside around five to ten minutes. This time should not be dependent on good behaviour. Remember not all child-centred time needs to be planned. Look for opportunities to spend time with your child throughout the day; reading in the morning before school, after school sitting and having a drink and a snack together or talking about their day.

Step two

'Special' time is one-on-one time. If you have other children in the family, it is important to find someone else (such as your spouse) to look after them, or choose a time when they are unlikely to disturb the activity.

Step three

Choose a time when you are able to relax and give your full attention to your child.

Step four

If you have a set time, you can say to your child, 'It's our special time to be together, what would you like to do?' Aim to have only a few toys or activities out at a time. Books, drawing materials and creative toys are particularly suited to child-centred time. If you do not have a special playtime, then approach your child whilst they are playing alone and ask if you can join in.

Step five

Try to avoid toys that encourage rough or aggressive play (such as bats, balls, boxing gloves); activities that could get out of hand (such as paints); and games that have pre-set rules. The aim is to set up a play situation that makes it easy for your child to behave calmly and considerately.

Step six

After watching your child's play for a couple of minutes, describe what they are doing (e.g., 'you are building a house', 'you're drawing a princess'). This shows the child that you are interested and will help to hold their attention.

Step seven

Look for opportunities to reflect your child's language (e.g., child: 'I'm drawing a clown with a red nose.' Parent: 'Yes, the clown has a red nose.' Child: 'I like to play with the doll's house.' Parent: 'It's a fun doll's house to play with.'). This shows your child that you are really listening and that you understand and accept what they are doing.

Step eight

After a while, join in by copying appropriate play (e.g., Child: 'I'm going to make a pizza.' Parent: 'I'm going to make some bread.' Child: 'I'm drawing a flower on my tree.' Parent: 'I'm going to draw a flower in my picture too.'). This shows your child that you are involved and teaches them to play with others.

Step nine

Find opportunities to acknowledge your child (e.g., 'that's an intricate picture', 'you're playing so quietly', 'thank you for sharing the pencils with me', 'I really enjoy it when we play together'). This adds to the warmth of the relationship and will help to increase your child's self-esteem.

Step ten

Avoid commands and questions during child-centered time. These prevent your child from leading the play and can make the playtime feel unpleasant.

Ignore inappropriate behaviour (e.g., talking back) unless it is dangerous or destructive. Do this by looking away for a moment. If your child engages in dangerous or destructive behaviour (e.g., hitting), tell them that the playtime is over and leave the room. Tell them that you will play later when they are able to participate appropriately. This avoids increasing inappropriate or inconsiderate behaviour (by withdrawing attention) and will help your child to see the difference in your response to considerate and inconsiderate behaviour.

Chapter 5

Giving instructions and choices

Parenting can be challenging, especially in terms of our skills, energy and emotions. We aim to establish relationships with our children that are both firm and caring so that we can meet as many of their needs as possible. This bond is often tested by our children when they try to determine how far they can go and how much power they have.

In establishing a loving relationship, it is vital that parents set reasonable boundaries to teach children what is appropriate and considerate behaviour. Children learn mostly through what they experience themselves rather than what they are told. This means that they will push the limits that you set to determine for themselves what they believe to be fair. In this sense, it is imperative that as parents we do and say the right things. This is not always easy, but it is essential we aim to practice it. If you are able to maintain these boundaries, you will be able to work better together and notice as the connection between you and your child improves. Confidence and commitment are important factors in ensuring that the boundaries you set have a positive influence on the relationship you have with your child.

Giving effective instructions

One of the most common errors made by parents is how they give instructions to their children. Typically, parents will issue an instruction and get no response. Then, apparently being ignored, they will repeat themseves in a variety of ways in order to get compliance. When the child continues to ignore, the parent eventually becomes angry and raises their voice, which in turn negatively reinforces the behaviour. The child learns to only respond when their parent is angry and loud. This locks both parties into a negative escalation trap.

Parents who get into the habit of using requests or giving instructions to children worded in a question format ('Can someone come and help with the dishes?'), are often frustrated and confused as to why their children don't listen. This is essentially because such phrases are non-committal and the child interprets the directive as a choice, which can be accepted or rejected as they wish. It is on the child's terms and we in turn get angry.

When we give clear instructions, children are more likely to comply. Clear instructions imply that an action is required: 'James, it's time to come and help with the dishes now.' There is an expectation that the child will act in accordance with what has been asked.

The typical escalation trap

Parent	Child	Parent Request
1. The parent makes a request	The child is not interested and/or may not hear. The request is perceived as a disturbance and the child ignores or does not acknowledge the instruction.	'James, can you please put away your toys?'

2. The parent repeats the request a second, third, fourth, and even fifth time. With each repetition, the request changes to pleading, bargaining, reasoning and threatening.	The child continues to ignore and pretends not to hear what is being requested. This habituation has occurred as they are so used to their parent talking in the background and have learnt to tune them out.	'James, are you listening to me?' 'Why aren't you being a good boy?' 'I'm getting fed up with waiting.' 'You had better do as you are told.' 'Those toys are still all over the room, and it's about time you put them away!'
3. Parent gets angry and demands that the child comply or face a punishment.	The child may argue, talk back, complain, whine, or run away and sulk/cry.	Parent with raised voice: 'Put those toys away.'
4. Parent loses their temper and pursues the issue, escalating their threats. At this point the parent is often emotional and distressed.	The child screams, cries, argues and throws a tantrum. Some children give in to this level of parental anger.	Parent shouting: 'Put those toys away now! Do you want me to throw them all in the bin.'

Typical requests made

Parent's request	Child's response
'Can you . . . ?'	'Umm, no. Since you asked.'
'Why don't you . . . ?'	'Because I don't want to.'

'You should . . .'	'I'll think about it. No, I don't think I will.'
'Don't you think . . . ?'	'No, actually . . .'
'Would you like . . . ?'	'No thanks . . .'
'I don't think . . .'	'Really? But I think something different.'
'It would be nice . . .'	'I suppose it would. But I'm still not going to.'
'How about . . . ?'	'No, it's OK.'
'I really wish you would . . .'	'That is nice to know.'
'Okay?'	'Maybe, but no. Since you asked.'

How to stop the escalation trap

To eliminate the 'escalation trap', it is imperative that parents delete all requests and choice statements from their vocabulary, particularly when there is no choice to be made. Parents need to help their child respond immediately instead of only when there is screaming and yelling involved. Parents need to be in control. You have the right to expect certain instructions are followed and that your child does the deeds that need to be done in an appropriate and considerate manner. To do all this with conviction, you need to maintain your role as the adult and your child's role as the child. Not the other way around. You need to listen to what your child says and make decisions that are fair and reasonable for your family, not decisions based on making the child happy. However, remember that children are more likely to accept a decision they do not like if they feel that you have listened and treated them fairly.

Elevating your child's position to level with yours may make them like you for a moment, but it does both of you no favours in the long run.

Wishy-washy phrases are the ladder on which your children climb to get to your level. It is much better to let them grow into the job.

Instructions need to be direct and clear; they must state what is expected in a certain situation. It is important that you give instructions to a new task once the child has stopped the current one; for example, turn off the television before you ask your child to clean their room, that way, their focus is on you and what you are asking them to do rather than on the television. If they ignore you or begin to demonstrate other challenging behaviour, you must act immediately.

It is important that children hear the instructions given. The best way to ensure that this happens is to go close to your child before speaking. Using your proximity and being an arm's length away ensures that they will hear what it is that you are requesting. Make sure that you give them enough time (five seconds) to follow through. If they still don't alter their behaviour or follow your instruction, then logical consequences can be implemented.

Simple steps for effective instruction giving

Step one
Use your proximity. Move closer and get to your child's level, an arm's length away is usually a good distance. It is also useful to use their name and make a connection with them.

Step two
Make sure that the instruction is to the point, clear and brief so that it is understood. For some children it helps to ask them to repeat the instruction and to acknowledge that they have understood: 'yes, that's right.'

Step three

If there is a list of instructions, break them down and give them one at a time.

Step four

Make sure your instruction is the last thing that they hear. If you need to explain anything, do this at the beginning; for example, 'Your grandmother is coming over for dinner, so we all need to help clean the house. You need to go and tidy your room now, please'.

Step five

Always use positive language when giving instructions; for example, 'walk inside the house' rather than 'don't run inside'.

Step six

Give your child time to cooperate (five seconds) and respond before you repeat the instruction.

Step seven

Avoid giving an instruction, leaving the room and then returning a period of time later to check.

Step eight

After giving an instruction stay focused on the task. Avoid distracting them from what you have asked them to do.

Step nine

Use labeled acknowledgement when your child follows an instruction. Describe exactly what they did well; for example, 'I felt so pleased to see you listening and getting dressed so quickly and cooperatively, thank you'.

Step ten

When instructions are not followed issue a choice statement and follow this by a logical consequence; for example, 'You need to put your shoes on before you can go to the park'.

Terminating instructions

As a parent it is best to use terminating instructions when your child is expressing aggression through such things as fighting, teasing, tormenting, and temper tantrums. Terminating instructions, can be used when asking a child to stop doing something; such as,' It is time for dinner. Turn off the television now, please'. In other cases, they can be used to address inconsiderate behaviour; such as: 'Yelling scares your brother. You need to use a quiet voice. Thank you.' Terminating instructions are also effective at times when house expectations are not followed, such as, 'we don't play sport inside, you need to take the ball outside and kick it in the backyard'.

Simple steps to delivering effective terminating instructions

Step one

Immediacy is important; as soon as you notice challenging behaviour, stop what you are doing and gain your child's attention by saying their name and getting down to their level. Start by asking 'what's happening?', 'what are you doing?' or 'what's going on?'

Step two

Clearly and firmly state what you want your child to do; for example, 'Jordan, what's happening? (Jordan responds with) 'nothing', 'then you need to start eating your dinner, thank you.'

Step three

Use descriptive acknowledgement when you child does what you've asked; for example, 'thanks for starting to eat your dinner.'

Step four

If your instruction is not followed, a logical consequence can be applied; for example, 'It's important to eat your dinner. Once you have eaten it . . . then you may have your dessert.'

Children quickly learn to cooperate when instructions are clear, respectful, firm and consistently delivered in a predictable manner. Appropriate consequences or giving choices are all about teaching children how to change and regulate their own behaviour. This will not occur overnight, but if you remain fair, firm, patient and consistent, you can avoid out-of-control arguments and damaging power struggles with your child.

Clear instruction sequence (to start a behaviour)

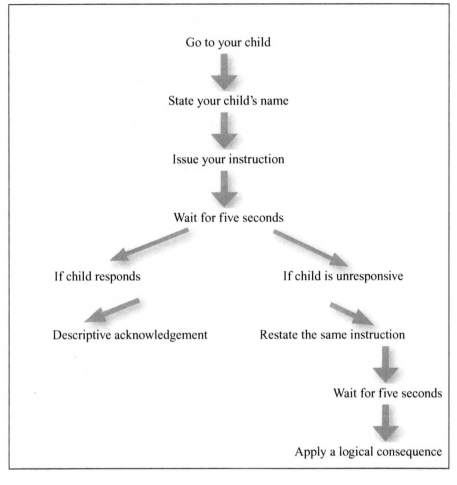

Adapted from Turner, Markie-Dadds & Sanders (1998)

Clear instruction sequence (to stop a behaviour)

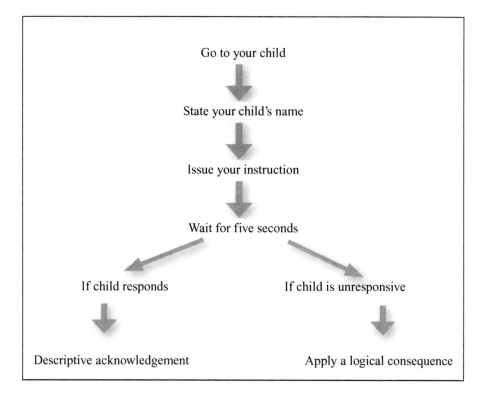

Go to your child

State your child's name

Issue your instruction

Wait for five seconds

If child responds

If child is unresponsive

Descriptive acknowledgement

Apply a logical consequence

Adapted from Turner, Markie-Dadds & Sanders (1998)

Parents need to be respectfully in charge. When parents are in charge, they are aware of their child's needs, are able to set fair limits and listen to their child's requests and questions. When parents are clear, calm, consistent and assertively in charge, children feel safe and secure. As parents, we need to listen to our children whilst remaining firm and loving in our expectations of them and their behaviour.

The in-charge parent

Parents

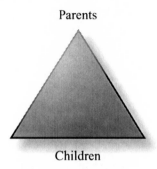

Children

Not the other way around.

Children

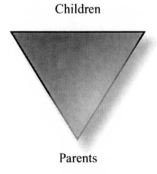

Parents

Remember, as parents we need to be thoughtful and courteous. After all, it is unreasonable to demand considerate behaviour from someone whom you do not always treat respectfully. You are your child's greatest teacher. The following formula is helpful when composing your instructions:

[insert task here]
+thank you

Or

[Child's name]
+ It is time to [insert task here]
+thank you

It is straightforward and effective, as long as you are prepared to follow through with consequences in cases of unresponsiveness. See how much more 'in charge' you could sound whilst being polite and specific with your instructions.

Examples of specific instructions

'Its time to come to the table for dinner now, please.'
'You need to keep your clothes folded neatly.'
'Do your homework when you get home, please.'
'It's time to leave the house, put your jacket on, thanks.'
'Speak politely using a calm voice, thank you.'
'We don't have time to change, you can wear what you have on, thanks.'
'Sam, it's time to pick up those toys and put them in the box, please.'
'Ben, it is time to come to the table for dinner now, please.'
'Kate, it's time to start your homework, thank you.'
'James, the program is over now, it's time to get ready for bed now, please.'

Consequences work well when they are approached through choice. For example, after your child does not respond to an instruction to pack away possessions you state, 'Remember our agreement that we tidy up after playing? Do you want to pack your Lego away now with my help or do you want to do it during your television time?' (Be aware that without adding a supportive statement 'with my help', the task may seem overwhelming to your child, resulting in a refusal to comply with your request).

It is important that you are consistent and follow through with any stated consequence. Not doing this will only confuse children. To avoid such situations remember your family's considerate behaviour agreements and the consequences that were agreed to when everyone was calm. This approach helps you to stay calm and to avoid making consequences that you can't or won't follow through with.

Implementing consequences isn't the only challenge; choosing them can also be difficult. When selecting a consequence, make sure that it is something that will work within your family, is realistic and can be followed through. Begin using consequences in one or two areas of your child's inconsiderate or problem behaviours. In this way you will not add unnecessary pressure by changing everything at once, and this will allow a smooth transition for your child into the new system. As you begin to follow through with consequences, you will notice that your child will start to follow instructions and will be better able to gain your attention in positive, rather than negative, ways.

Using choices with your child

Choices enable children to develop decision-making skills. They also allow them to understand consequences through taking responsibility. Choices are important, especially as your child gets older, as making choices allows children to feel as though they get a say in their lives, even if it is only on a small scale. This provides an opportunity for them to feel as though they are in control, and they are therefore more likely to comply which will limit your frustration as a parent.

Choice statements

While choice is important, parents still need to be clear on their expectations. An effective use of choice could be: 'Would you prefer to do your piano practice now or after dinner?' This sort of statement is structured around what you need your child to do but has given them some power with regard to when to do it.

Effective choice strategies:

- **An either or choice**—'You can either have cereal or toast.'
- **A sequence choice**—'What would you prefer to do first? Your homework or the dishes?'

- **A time choice**—'Would you prefer to start your project now or wait until 5 p.m.?'
- **Multiple choice**—'Would you prefer to wear your coat, carry it, or put on a jumper?'
- **Advanced warning**—'In five minutes it will be bed time.'

A when-then statement

A when-then statement is another positive way to express your requirements. When-then statements tell your child what they need to do before moving on to what they want to do. 'When your books are picked up off the floor, then I will read the rest of our story.' Statements such as these, gives your child the power to bring about a certain result, while you maintain control.

Building your bag of tricks

How to make instructions effective

Step One
Clearly state instructions in a calm and friendly manner. Remember, not to make your instruction a question.

Step Two
Give your instruction twice to start a behaviour and once to stop a behaviour.

Step Three
Wait for five seconds before repeating instructions.

Step Four
If repeating an instruction, state exactly what you stated previously.

Step Five

Do not make instructions too long or complex. If you want your child to do several things, state the first instruction, and then, when it has been completed, move on to the next, etc.

Step Six

Make sure that you state your child's name and are within an arm's length of them. Do not yell instructions from another room.

Step Seven

Ask your child to repeat the instruction if necessary.

Step Eight

Only give choices if there is a choice to be made.

Chapter 6

Consequences

As parents, we sometimes ask our children questions like 'why do you never listen to me?' This is often an attempt to understand why they act in certain ways, especially when their behaviour is challenging. It can come over as an accusation, inadvertently creating greater hostility in the relationship between parent and child. This sort of situation often comes about when a parent feels frustrated or angry and wants to ensure their child knows how bad they are feeling. This is a negative and unhelpful approach, which at worst can become abusive as anger and frustration increase.

These 'why' questions are problematic because children can rarely provide an answer. Therefore they often reply with an 'I don't know' or respond by getting upset. This response does not ease the situation and often just intensifies your feelings. It also creates a situation where the child feels as though whatever they say or do will be inadequate or wrong. A more effective way of addressing behaviours that you are not happy with is by using consequences or 'I' statements, as discussed earlier (Chapter 2).

In cases where you believe your child is aware of the reasons behind their behaviour, ask them to verbalise it. Start by asking them what happened or what was going on. A good time for a discussion like this is when you are both calm. Children often want to share their feelings with someone that they care for in a safe and accepting environment. Be sure not to raise questions in an angry tone immediately after the incident in question, it is best to wait for the right moment when everyone is back in control.

Avoiding arguments

It is not possible to be an 'in charge' parent when arguing with your child. When feeling hurt, frustrated, or angry it is difficult to stop yourself from engaging in an immature and destructive situation, but this will not lead to resolution of the problem. When you do take part in arguments at your child's level, you open yourself up to being unable to:

- act as a positive role model
- gain and maintain respect
- address the problem in a constructive manner.

Reduce negative emotional expression

Shouting is often an approach used by parents when they are frustrated or angry. It may work in the beginning but as time progresses children become accustomed to this strategy and tend to stop responding. This habituation tends to lead to an escalation with no long-term improvement in behaviour, or worse—cooperation only when we display this level of aggression and loss of temper. The same occurs when smacking is used as a form of punishment or a strategy. These are not effective methods of parenting, as they do not form good long-term patterns of behaviour and often result in children becoming oppositional. A child will respond better if they view their parent as rational, calm, respectful and loving.

Ask yourself this simple question

> Do you want your child to do as you ask because they are afraid
> or because it is the right thing to do?

Another important factor in limiting the expression of negative emotions is to model respectful communication within the parental relationship. Children are unable to feel calm and safe when their parents are hostile towards each other. Parents need to act as role models so children learn how to deal with conflict and behave appropriately. This behaviour will be projected on to other people in their life such as parents, peers and other adults. Modelling based on the example of highly conflicted parents often causes children problems in future relationships.

When children become aware of arguments within their home, they not only worry about the prospect of separation and having to choose sides, but may also feel that they are responsible for the conflict. All parents disagree from time to time and it is healthy for a child to know this, but they must see that you address any issues in a considerate way.

Planned ignoring

One of the most powerful techniques available to parents is the use of their attention. In general terms, pay extra attention to any behaviour you want to see repeated in your child and ignore negative behaviours. Obviously you cannot ignore dangerous or serious behaviour, but planned ignoring can be very effective for the annoying little things children do—particularly if they are doing it in order to get an emotional response.

Planned ignoring works when you withdraw eye contact immediately and have no verbal or physical contact. Don't make a big show of it, act like the behaviour is simply not happening. Give your full awareness immediately when the negative behaviour stops and make a positive comment that acknowledges the more desirable behaviour. Some parents prefer to signal their intention to ignore, for example, 'I cannot talk to you when you yell at me, you need to use a calm voice'. This strategy teaches children that they cannot get your attention by doing irritating and inconsiderate things. They learn that acting in a reasonable and considerate way brings your attention and positive feedback.

Consequences

Consequences can be divided into two categories: natural and pre-agreed. Our wider environment determines natural consequences, such as if you throw a ball near a tree, it will probably get stuck. These sorts of consequences revolve around the idea of cause and effect. Being able to deal with natural consequences becomes more and more essential as a child gets older. They need these skills throughout their development into their adult self. In allowing your child to acquire these skills, it is important that you allow the likely process to occur without always rescuing them from the consequence.

Pre-agreed consequences are fair responses to inconsiderate or undesirable behaviour, which are discussed and agreed to by both parent and child. These consequences should be designed for each individual child in accordance with age and developmental level and they should be followed through with as little expression of negative emotion as possible (i.e., avoid shouting, sighing, anger/ frustration).

Logical consequences

Logical consequences are an effective way to manage your child's inconsiderate behaviour. Logical consequences are not designed to be a punishment, but rather they are meant to teach children that their inconsiderate conduct was an error rather than a 'felony'. They are designed to give children the skills to be responsible for their own actions.

Logical consequences should be based around dealing with behaviour when it happens, rather than including all past events in the way that punishment often does. The implementation of logical consequences needs to be kind and firm and can be introduced as choices; for example, 'If you keep leaving the dinner table, I will think that you have finished eating and I will take your food away'. If you are consistent in the application of consequences, your child will learn to correct their own behaviour.

Logical consequences are about teaching children how to change and regulate their own behaviour. Change in behaviour will not occur overnight, but if you remain firm, patient and consistent, you can avoid out-of-control arguments and damaging power struggles with your child. Below is a step-by-step guide of how to effectively use logical consequences.

Logical consequences—the steps

Step one
Give your instruction in an effective way (as discussed previously).

Step two
If your instruction is ignored, follow through with a logical consequence. It is important that the logical consequence matches the behavioural error; for example, if your child doesn't put their plate in the dishwasher before it is put on, then state they need to wash it by hand in the sink.

Step three
Explain the consequence and do not argue the point.

Step four
Once the instruction has been followed, discuss with your child what should occur next time.

Step five

Repeat the logical consequence if the behaviour recurs and follow up with some quiet time if required.

Ideas for consequences:

- Planned ignoring
- Removal of the problem toy or object for a short amount of time (five to thirty minutes' works best)
- Cool down
- Restoration—making things better (e.g., saying sorry, earning money to pay for a broken item, doing something nice for the other person . . .)
- Practicing appropriate behaviour (e.g., repeating the request in an appropriate voice)

The main aim of logical consequences is to teach children how to make good choices through experience. Consequences need to be kept brief and realistic so that you can follow through with them, and your child can both learn and practice the correct behaviour.

Cool Down

Cool Down is the next step of consequences if your child does not respond to your limit setting or when their behaviour has escalated to a point where they cannot respond to any direction or instruction. Cool Down is a structured management tool designed to help children learn to manage their own behaviour and to calm down. Children learn to regulate their anger on their own and this leads to a spacious and flexible window of tolerance.

Cool Down is designed to interrupt the child in the midst of behaving inconsiderately, removing them to a designated spot. Then the parent completely removes their attention. The child is only allowed to leave Cool Down when they have calmed down.

Remember, children strive for parents' attention whether it is positive or negative. Removing your attention immediately when your child begins to behave in unacceptable ways is an extremely effective means of changing that particular behaviour.

Cool Down is useful when a child is totally out of their window of tolerance and unable to manage their emotions. In such a state, they cannot respond to verbal instructions. At these times, the aim is to have your child calm down to a point where they are able to respond.

The key with Cool Down is to be clear and consistent. The most powerful form of reinforcement is intermittent reinforcement. That is, if you respond to inconsiderate behaviour inconsistently, you can expect that particular behaviour to be more stubborn to eliminate. Your children will continually invite you to be consistent and offer you more opportunities to be consistent in your implementation of reinforcement and consequences.

Before getting started:

- choose a Cool Down spot that lacks stimulation—the Cool Down spot is a space for the child to cool down. This could be a particular chair or step. It is a good idea to mark this out with a sticker to preclude arguments.
- remember to run through all the steps with your child before you implement this strategy
- make sure that you have a timer that can be used for Cool-Down.

Cool Down steps

Step one
Give a clear and calm instruction without expressed anger; for example, 'Stop screaming, you need to calm down'.

Step two
Within five seconds, give a warning: 'This is your warning. You need to . . . (restate what you have just asked your child to do or stop doing).' Stay calm and do not add extra instruction.

Step three
If your child does not respond within five to twenty seconds, state: 'You need to go to Cool Down' in a firm but not angry voice. From this point on, do not talk to your child, make eye contact, or express anger or any other emotion.

Step four
Place your child in Cool Down. You may need to physically guide them to the Cool Down area.

Step five
Set the timer.

Step six
Allow your child to leave when the timer rings, if the child has been settled for at least ten seconds. If the child has not been settled for at least ten seconds when the timer goes off, calmly say: 'You were not quiet/calm when the timer went off, so now you need to stay there until you have been quiet/calm for half a minute'. Reset the timer and walk away calmly (the goal is to not reinforce the disruptive behaviour).

The key to the effectiveness of Cool Down is in how quickly you act; the quicker you act the better the response. Cool Down allows your child to understand that consequences increase if their behaviour does not improve or in fact gets worse. Cool Down allows other family members to have some time to calm down too.

Some children may need their parent to sit close by and provide supportive statements such as; 'you're calming down now', 'you need to breath slowly', 'when you're calm you can . . .', 'you can do this, calming down now . . .'.

Post-incident discussion

It is important that once your child has finished their Cool Down, that you have a discussion about what happened, who was affected, what they need to do to make things right and what could have been done differently. This allows your child to understand that when they make mistakes they are able to make things right (to restore their relationship) and learn to take responsibility for their actions. It is vital that this discussion also offers acknowledgement for what they did well so as not to focus solely on the negative. For example, 'Once you went to the kitchen for Cool Down, you sat quietly and when you returned to the game we were playing, you got involved in a really positive way; you waited your turn and you shared'.

Techniques to avoid with children

Threatening—when a child continues to ignore instructions parents will often get angry and respond with a consequence that they cannot follow through with. Consequences should be kept simple, realistic and immediate; for example, 'You are still ignoring me, so I am turning off the television until . . .'

Nagging—many parents find that their nagging leads to empty threats and causes frustration and anger; for example, a parent may ask their child to do their homework. Although the child isn't doing it, and the parent continues to ask them, with frustration showing in their tone each time they are ignored. These escalation traps can be avoided by remembering the rule of thumb for instruction giving (two instructions to start a behaviour and one to stop) and remaining calm and clear in your expectations; for example, 'You need to start your homework in five minutes once the television show you are watching has finished.' Ensure that you get a response. When you come back in five minutes and notice a new show is on, you need to give more guidance; for example, get their homework out of their bag and bring it over to them, calmly turn off the television and say, 'Today, it looks like its just your spelling list, ten maths questions, and a home reader. How about we do the spelling and maths now and leave the reader until bedtime?' This ensures that not too many tasks are done at once and that they are manageable. It is important that you acknowledge your child while they are doing the task with a greater focus on effort rather than on the end result.

Humiliation/sarcasm—when frustrated with a child's behaviour some parents find themselves making statements about their child's character rather than their behaviour; for example, 'you're careless' or 'you're mean'. When this occurs, especially in front of others, children feel as though this is who they are. If something is said often enough, a child will begin to act accordingly. This sort of language and behaviour can also create greater hostility and rivalry between siblings, which may result in setting up the other children to take the fall.

Parent control/intrusion—in challenging situations parents can at times respond by becoming stricter with their children. However, control and intrusion leads to strong resistance.

Building your bag of tricks

The following bag of tricks will assist you in positive long-lasting change in the interaction you have with your child. These will not have a noticeable effect immediately, but with time and commitment, the change will occur.

Good guide to parenting tips

Tip one—be consistent
By your being consistent, your child knows what they are expected to do and what happens if they behave inconsiderately.

Tip two—making promises
If you make promises, be careful to ensure they are something you can keep. Sometimes you will need to change your decisions on certain things but make sure that you explain the reasons for change to your child.

Tip three—consequences
Punishment is unwise, use consequences. Consequences must not be humiliating, they should relate to the inconsiderate behaviour and should be followed through with as soon as possible. The withdrawal or limiting of affection should never be used.

Tip four—follow through
Mean what you say and act on it. Threats of consequences are not nearly as effective as following through with a discussed consequence. Remember, children learn best from experiencing something themselves.

Tip five—expectations
Ensure that the expectations you have for your child's behaviour are reasonable for their age and capability.

Tip six—acknowledgement
Ensure that you acknowledge considerate behaviour when it occurs more frequently instead of just implementing consequences when inconsiderate actions occur.

Chapter 7

Releasing children from playing roles

Allowing your child to view themselves differently is an important part of being a parent. There are simple ways that parents can help children to be free from playing the roles they have become accustomed to. Below are seven tips on how to do this:

Tip one
Try to find opportunities to allow your child to see a new side of themselves; for example, 'I noticed you sharing your chocolate bar with your little brother even though I know you were looking forward to eating it all. Thank you'.

Tip two
Create situations where your child can get a different perspective; for example, 'I have to start making dinner now, keep writing your story as you're doing a great job there all by yourself'.

Tip three

Allow your child to hear you saying positive things about them to other people; for example, 'Today, Maya got dressed and packed her bag all by herself, it was such a great help as we were running late'.

Tip four

Make sure that you are setting the example that you would like your children to follow.

Tip five

Even if your child may not be practicing considerate behaviour all the time, it is important that you acknowledge them when they are trying.

Tip six

Remind your child of the special moments or the good things they have done. This shows them that you care and will encourage them to do it again; for example, 'I still smile when I think about that time your teacher called me to tell me about how helpful you were at the athletics carnival'.

Tip seven

When your child starts to slip back into their old label, such as lazy, mean, rude, etc., you need to tell them how this makes you feel, and what you expect from them now; for example, 'Sarah, your room is looking very messy lately. I get frustrated when I have to pick up after you. You need to keep you room tidy'.

Managing sibling conflict

When parents frequently get drawn into their children's arguments, everyone in the family is affected. Parents become exhausted and frustrated from the pressure to referee and resolve every argument and children become resentful towards each other and their parents. In addition, when parents are dragged into arguments they give attention to the problematic behaviour and deprive children of the opportunity to learn to negotiate and compromise. When parents intervene and give their children attention when they are fighting and then fail to acknowledge the times when they are getting along well, children subconsciously learn that a good way to get attention from their parents is to squabble and fight.

Teach your children the skills they need to deal with each other and then support them to sort conflict out amongst themselves. For example, when they are fighting over a toy, take the toy and put it on the table saying, 'I know the two of you can work this out. Now you need to sit here and talk about it. You're capable of solving this problem without me.'

To encourage positive play:

- Acknowledge and draw attention to cooperative play and sharing; for example, 'you are playing so well together' and 'it's great when we build things together'.
- Acknowledge children as a team for conflict-free periods; for example, 'thank you for playing together quietly while I was making dinner.'
- Spend time with each child individually, as well as together

When arguments occur:

- Avoid listening to one child telling tales about the other—encourage children to work things out between themselves if possible.
- If an argument needs to be stopped, do not try to work out who started it—rather, ask each child in the presence of the other what happened.

- Apply consequences to children as a team; for example, remove a toy or turn off the television if the children can't work it out together

Managing high-risk situations

Before the situation:

- When scheduling a trip or visit, try to organise it to fit in with current sleeping and eating habits of the child and general family.
- Make sure that you manage your time effectively so that it does not cause excessive stress or rushing. This is especially important when getting ready to go out.
- Explain to your child what is going on, whether it will be a quick trip to the shops, a few family members coming over for dinner, or a long drive or plane trip. Make sure you allow them to ask any questions they have and that you answer them.
- Review expectations with your child beforehand. Be specific about considerate behaviour.
- Make sure that your child is aware of the expectations. Ask your child to say them back to you to ensure they are aware of them.
- Discuss with your child what the consequences will be for considerate behaviour ('we will be able to stay longer') and for inconsiderate behaviour ('we will have to leave early').
- Agree on two or three engaging activities and prepare to implement these if your child gets bored or restless.

In the situation:

- Notice your child behaving considerately and acknowledge this behaviour.
- Watch out for boredom and be ready with alternative activities if needed. In situations such as when visitors come to dinner, make

sure that you give your child attention now and again and make sure you include them.
- When your child begins to behave inconsiderately, immediately gain their attention and redirect their behaviour.
- If the behaviour continues, give a firm but calm instruction and a reminder that the consequences discussed will be implemented if the considerate behaviour occurs (i.e., 'we will be able to stay longer').
- If the inconsiderate behaviour continues, then follow through with the consequence discussed for inconsiderate behaviour (i.e., 'we will have to leave early').
- Where possible, use your humour and even turn the situation into a game; for example, if you are cleaning up, you could say 'okay let's see how quickly we can clean up'.

Calming strategies

When children are out of control, there is no use in stating consequences because they are out of their window of tolerance and are unable to respond. They can not process what has been said. At these times children need assistance to self regulate and calm.

Step one—remain calm
You cannot help your child to calm when you are out of control.

Step two—label your child's behaviour
'Sarah you are out of control.'

Step three—go to your child and speak calmly
'I am going to help you to calm down'. You may have to hold them, hug them, rock them, or quietly sing to them.

Step four—move your child away

If necessary, move your child from the problem situation so that there is not an audience and so that your calming attempts are successful.

Step five—rest

After your child has calmed they are likely to be very tired and may need to rest or engage in a calm activity with you; for example, drawing, reading a book or going for a walk

Even if your child is lacking self-control, you can still focus on considerate behaviour once they are calm. Have a follow up conversation with your child and ask 'what happened?', 'who was effected?', 'how can you make this right?' and 'what could we do differently next time?'. You may need to plan ahead for the high risk situation and/or modify the situation. Make sure that you end this process by reconnection and by acknowledging your child for what they did considerately and for calming down.

Chapter 8

Pulling it all together—your bag of tricks

When deciding what strategies to put into your 'bag of tricks', remember that you know your family situation inside out. By being clear in your goals for your family, you can make your parenting role easier. This 'bag of tricks' approach is about not tolerating intolerable behaviour, rather it is about positively guiding children's behaviour. These tricks are designed to guide, as opposed to control, children and stem from the acknowledgement that children, by virtue of being children, will make behavioural errors. These powerful strategies appeal to children's pride, reason, logic and concern for others.

Your bag of tricks may include:

Tips for encouraging considerate behaviour

- consider your child's needs and respond to them when necessary
- spend time with your child individually, doing things that they like to do
- talk to them, ask questions, and take an interest in their play, games and friends

- acknowledge their accomplishments and appropriate behaviour
- cuddle, laugh, and have fun with your child often
- encourage independence by allowing your child to do things to help you and others
- listen and respond to your child when they ask for your help, information, advice, or opinion, or when they want to tell you something
- provide a good language model for your child (i.e., avoid baby talk)
- provide lots of interesting and stimulating books, toys, games and activities to encourage play, talking and intellectual stimulation
- model considerate behaviours that you want to encourage in your child (e.g., helping others, being a good listener, using a pleasant voice, taking care of your belongings, being friendly, cheerful and interested in others)
- guide the family, rather than having either an 'anything goes' attitude or insisting on being the boss
- use natural consequences for considerate behaviour; for example, when a child says 'thank you', instead of saying 'good girl', say 'you're welcome' or 'it's a pleasure' or give them a hug
- establish guidelines that define considerate behaviour; for example, the house expectation that everyone keeps their hands and feet to themselves. Guidelines help make your responses predictable over time and leave you free to decide how to respond, depending on the circumstances.
- regard behavioural mistakes as natural—remember that thoughtless behaviour occurs because children are unable to behave like adults that they have to learn how to behave considerately. It is your job as a parent to teach this complex skill to your child.
- modify your demands—when children's actions indicate that they cannot cope, you can change what you expect of them
- be assertive about inconsiderate behaviour by telling children what the effect of their behaviour is having, without blaming or criticising them

- guide children to solve their problems collaboratively when they are in conflict
- give children choices when choices can be made—if there is no choice, you can ask your child how they would like to do it (e.g., when)
- be wise in your decision-making—it is okay to be flexible and change your mind as long as you are not allowing intolerable behaviour
- teach self-control when children are out of control—most tantruming children know how to behave but are temporarily overwhelmed by their feelings and cannot act on that information

Have a stepladder of tricks in your bag; for example, humour, acknowledgement, effective instruction delivery, choice statements, logical consequences and then Cool Down only when necessary. The strategy must be appropriate to the degree of inconsiderate and inappropriate behaviour.

Tips for discouraging inconsiderate behaviour

- remain calm when speaking to a child who is upset or has behaved inconsiderately—avoid becoming angry when your child is upset; speak calmly but firmly
- respond to inconsiderate behaviour immediately, consistently, and decisively. Act, rather than threatening to act. Deal with the problem yourself, rather than threatening someone else's action.
- set limits to your child's behaviour—do not give in and accidentally reinforce or encourage your child for being inconsiderate (e.g., when they demand or whine)
- avoid responding to inconsiderate behaviour by trying to distract your child
- respond to inconsiderate behaviour by telling your child what to do as opposed to what not to do (e.g., say 'use a calm voice', rather

than saying, 'stop yelling'). Try to avoid unclear instructions or requests (e.g., 'don't be silly').

- back up your instructions by using choice statements, natural or logical consequences and Cool Down

- discuss expectations with your child and give them a chance to be involved in deciding on the family expectations and consequences

- prevent problems by ensuring that your child has plenty of interesting and engaging things to do

- keep a look out for when your child is behaving considerately and make sure you acknowledge it. Expectations can be linked to a personal quality, such as 'I saw you helping your sister with her spelling; that was really helpful'.

- remember, to choose your battles—focus on your target behaviour(s)

- children's feelings should always be acknowledged, especially when they are feeling upset, anxious, angry or frustrated. It is important that you are very clear that even when a child is feeling this way, it is never okay for them to act out with violence. You need to teach your child that all of these feelings are okay, but it is not okay to express these feelings through verbal or physical aggression. In giving this message, it may be helpful to give them other strategies to manage their strong feelings. Some strategies include taking time to calm down, have a run around or doing another form of exercise, channeling your anger into something else, such as yelling into a pillow, stomping, clapping, blowing bubbles or scribbling on a piece of paper. It can helpful for a child to write down what has made them angry so that once they are calm, you can discuss what happened and why they felt the way they did.

- in a situation where a child makes a behavioural error and acts inconsiderately, it is important to acknowledge the child's feelings, explain the boundaries in regards to the situation, and reiterate what the considerate behaviour is for the situation. Verbal responses should be as brief as possible.

- consistency is vital—children will push poorly defined boundaries. If you are finding it difficult to be consistent with the expectations that you have set, then you may need to review them. Sometimes difficulties arise because an expectation is too restrictive, not age or developmentally appropriate or a child does not have the physical or intellectual capabilities to comply with the expectation. Keep your expectations reasonable and persist. It may be challenging in the beginning, but you will find that your parenting role gets easier.

- once your child reaches five or six years of age involving them in discussing and agreeing on family expectations becomes more important. It is a good idea to sit your child down and talk with them at a calm time, where you both are feeling good and rational. You should discuss the expectations that you want to have in place and ways you can incorporate their growing needs for privacy, control and responsibility of their own lives. Get your child's input into what the consequences should be for inconsiderate behaviour.

- immediacy in giving acknowledgement and consequences is key to their effectiveness

- as parents, we should aim to use 'natural' consequences as much as possible, especially as children move towards the teenage years. These can occur in many situations, for instance, if a child refuses to take their jacket to school, they will get cold. If a child uses their pencils too roughly, then they will break. In these sorts of cases, the 'natural' consequences provide a strong enough message to your child without you needing to add any extra consequence.

- children need to be given elements of control in their day-to-day life and a good tool to enable this is choice. The development of choice strategies is important as it becomes more and more necessary as children reach the teenage years. In teaching your child about negotiation and compromise, you are developing skills which will make them more likely to accept and comply with fair expectations and more able to make good choices.

- avoid being confrontational with your children as much as you can
- when parents issue effective instructions, children no longer ignore requests
- only make a request or instruction that you are prepared to enforce
- issue effective instructions—go to your child and state their name rather than yelling an instruction from across the room
- be specific with instructions so that there is little room for misunderstanding; for example, instead of saying 'go away', if you need the child to leave the kitchen as you are cooking at the stove and it is hot, you should say, 'it is not safe to play games in the kitchen. Go and play in the lounge room, thank you'. While in the short term, all of these additions to giving an instruction may be tiring, it will result in a positive long-term effect of establishing healthy habits in your child in regards to listening and following instructions.

As a parent, it is important that we steer away from threatening, nagging, shouting, verbal aggression and humiliating behaviour directed at children. While we all are aware of this, we can find ourselves slipping into these patterns when we are feeling stressed, tired, angry, or frustrated and it's unrealistic to expect you'll get things right all the time. Nevertheless, if you take the ideas outlined in this book and build your skills over time, you will find that the moments of frustration and exhaustion become less and less. Following the recommendations and suggestions in this book will help you to develop considerate, sensible and independent young people. Your relationship with your child will be nurtured and you will be able to experience more of the joy and richness our children bring to our lives.

References

Pantley, E. (2000). *Hidden messages*. USA: Contemporary Books.

Porter, L. (2001). Children are people too: A parent's guide to young children's behaviour. SA: Small Poppies.

Seligman. (1995). *The Optimistic Child*. Australia: Random House.

Turner, K.M.T., Markie-Dadds, C., & Sanders, M.R. (1998). *Facilitator's manual for Group Triple P.* Brisbane, QLD, Australia: Families International Publishing.

CPSIA information can be obtained at www.ICGtesting.com
Printed in the USA
LVOW08s0228210616

493459LV00001B/45/P